BATTY RIDDLES

by Katy Hall and Lisa Eisenberg

pictures by Nicole Rubel

PUFFIN BOOKS

PUFFIN BOOKS
Published by the Penguin Group
Penguin Putnam Inc., 375 Hudson Street, New York, New York 10014, U.S.A.
Penguin Books Ltd, 27 Wrights Lane, London W8 5TZ, England
Penguin Books Australia Ltd, Ringwood, Victoria, Australia
Penguin Books Canada Ltd, 10 Alcorn Avenue, Toronto, Ontario, Canada M4V 3B2
Penguin Books (N.Z.) Ltd, 182-190 Wairau Road, Auckland 10, New Zealand

Penguin Books Ltd, Registered Offices: Harmondsworth, Middlesex, England

First published in the United States of America by Dial Books for Young Readers,
a division of Penguin Books USA Inc., 1993
Published in a Puffin Easy-to-Read edition, 1997

1 3 5 7 9 10 8 6 4 2

Text copyright © Katy Hall and Lisa Eisenberg, 1993
Pictures copyright © Nicole Rubel, 1993
All rights reserved
Puffin® and Easy-to-Read® are registered trademarks of Penguin Putnam Inc.

THE LIBRARY OF CONGRESS HAS CATALOGED THE DIAL EDITION AS FOLLOWS:
Hall, Katy. Batty riddles/
by Katy Hall and Lisa Eisenberg ; pictures by Nicole Rubel.
p. cm.
Summary: A collection of riddles about bats, including "Why did the little bat
walk around in his pajamas? He didn't have a bat robe!"
ISBN 0-8037-1217-0. ISBN 0-8037-1218–9 (lib. bdg.)
1. Riddles—Juvenile. 2. Bats—Juvenile humor. [1. Bats—Wit and humor. 2. Riddles.]
I. Eisenberg, Lisa. II. Rubel, Nicole, ill. III. Title.
PN6371.5.H345 1993 818'.5402—dc20 91-20777 CIP AC

Puffin Easy-to-Read ISBN 0-14-038724-2
Printed in the United States of America

Reading Level 1.8

To all the kids who drive us batty—
Leigh, Kate, Annie, and Tommy
K.H. and L.E.

To my Batty husband
N.R.

What do you get if you cross
a vampire and a big dance?

A bat ball!

Why did the vampire bat's girlfriend break up with him?

She thought
he was a pain in the neck!

What did the little bat say
when she was asked to dinner?

"No fangs, I just ate!"

Why did the little bat
walk around in his pajamas?

He didn't have a bat robe!

Why did the little bat
use mouthwash?

She had bat breath!

When do bats squeak?

When they need to be oiled!

What famous flying mammal
lived in ancient Egypt?

Cleobatra!

Why did Junior Bat
want to get a job?

He was tired
of just hanging around.

Why did the baseball player strike out?

He was using the wrong bat!

What did the little bat
do in school when she didn't
know the answer?

She just winged it!

Why did Mom Bat
hate the letter "r"?

Because it turned
her baby into a brat!

What fruit do
vampires like best?

Neck-tarines.

Where are you most likely
to find bats in your house?

In the bat-room.

What do you get if
you cross a ball with a bat?

A home run!

What bat invaded Europe?

Battilla the Hun!

Where do bats go to gamble?

Batlantic City!

Which bat hangs the highest?

The acro-bat!

What happened when the
little bat swallowed
the doorbell?

It turned into a dingbat!

What is a vampire's favorite animal?

The giraffe.

What kind of car does a vampire drive?

A bloodmobile!

Why did the vampire
cross the road?

It was attached to
the chicken's neck!

What do you get when
you cross a frog and
a flying mammal?

A creature that says,
"Ribbat, ribbat!"

What game do baby vampires like to play?

Batty cake, batty cake!

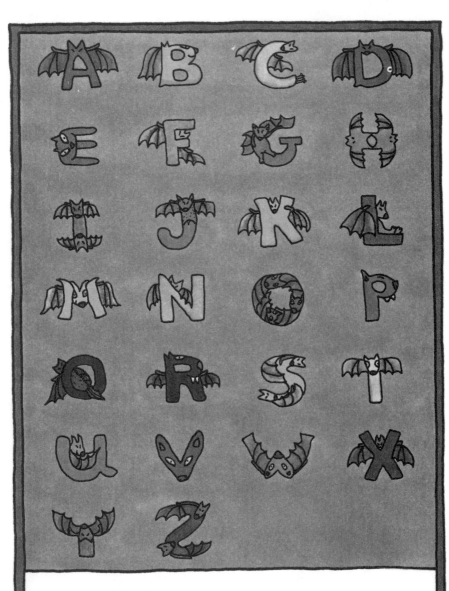

Which bat knows its ABCs?

The alpha-bat!

What do you get if you cross
a bat and a hatchet?

A battle-ax!

What bat makes
your camera work?

The bat-tery!

What holiday do
bats love best?

St. Batrick's Day!

Why couldn't the little vampire play baseball?

He was only a bat boy!

What do you get
if you cross a vampire
with a snowflake?

Frostbite!

What flying mammal might
you find in a Paris church?

The Hunchbat of Notre Dame.

What position did the little vampire play on the football team?

Quarterbat.

What do you have to know
to teach a bat tricks?

More than the bat!

What do you call a dream
about a vampire chasing you?

A bitemare!

What kind of dogs
do vampires like best?

Bloodhounds!

What game do little batties
like to play with little birdies?

Batminton!

Why didn't the little bat
laugh at the joke about
the cave?

It was too deep for him!

Why should you never let
a vampire into your car?

It'll drive you batty!

What do you get if you cross
a bat with a woodpecker?

Bat-a-tat-tat!

What bat hero wears a cape
and can leap tall buildings
in a single bound?

Swooperman!

What do you call vampires
that cheer you on
at football games?

Bat-on twirlers!

What bat sewed
the American flag?

Batsy Ross!

What do you say when you come to the end of *Batty Riddles?*

"Bat's all, Folks!"